THE ULTIMATE MONEY WORKBOOK FOR TEENS

Disclaimer: The information on this website is for general information only.
It should not be taken as constituting professional advice.

I am not a financial adviser. You should consider seeking independent legal, financial, taxation or other advice to check how the website information relates to your unique circumstances.

Pretty Pickles is not liable for any loss caused, whether due to negligence or otherwise arising from the use of, or reliance on, the information provided directly or indirectly, by use of this website.

Introduction

It's true that money will not buy you happiness but having smart money management skills can set you up for financial freedom, giving you the option to spend your time doing things you love.

If you're reading this, congratulations! There's no better time to build your financial
skills than now. That's because the earlier you start, the more time you'll have to let your money work hard for you. You'll also have time to recover from any money mistakes you make.

If this is your first book about finance and money management, this book will cover all the basics you need to know. By the time you finish the book, you'll be able to

- Develop a strong, resilient money mindset
- Create a budget you can stick to
- Have a financial plan that sets you up for your goals
- Create a long term investment strategy

CHAPTER ONE
Money Mindset

Your Values

What we value is directly related to how we spend our money and time. For example, someone who values their family will spend their time and money with/on their family. Whereas, someone who values their career might spend their time studying or investing their money into more education. When it comes to values, there are seven pillars of life to consider:

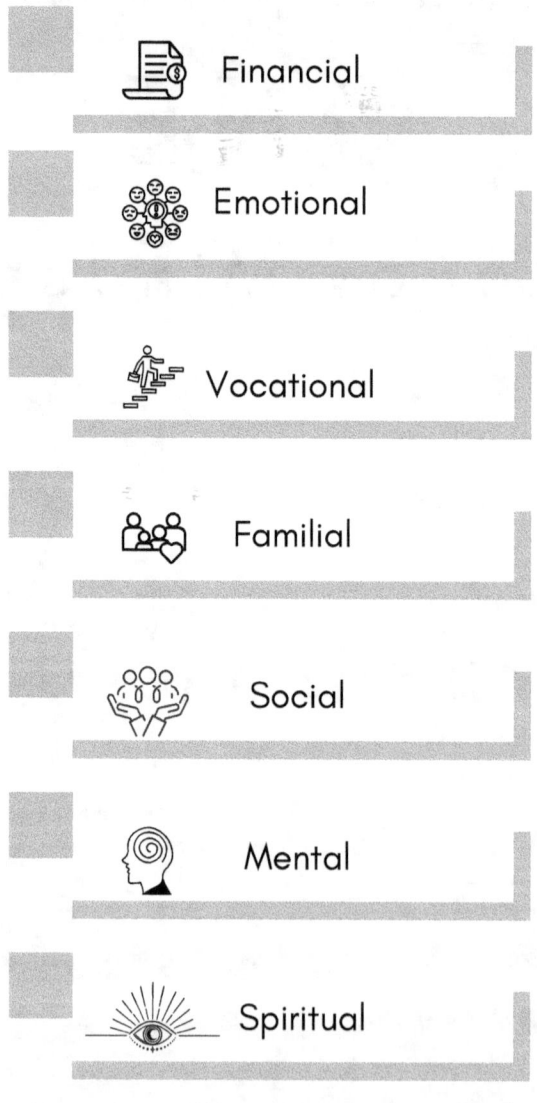

- Financial
- Emotional
- Vocational
- Familial
- Social
- Mental
- Spiritual

What do you value?

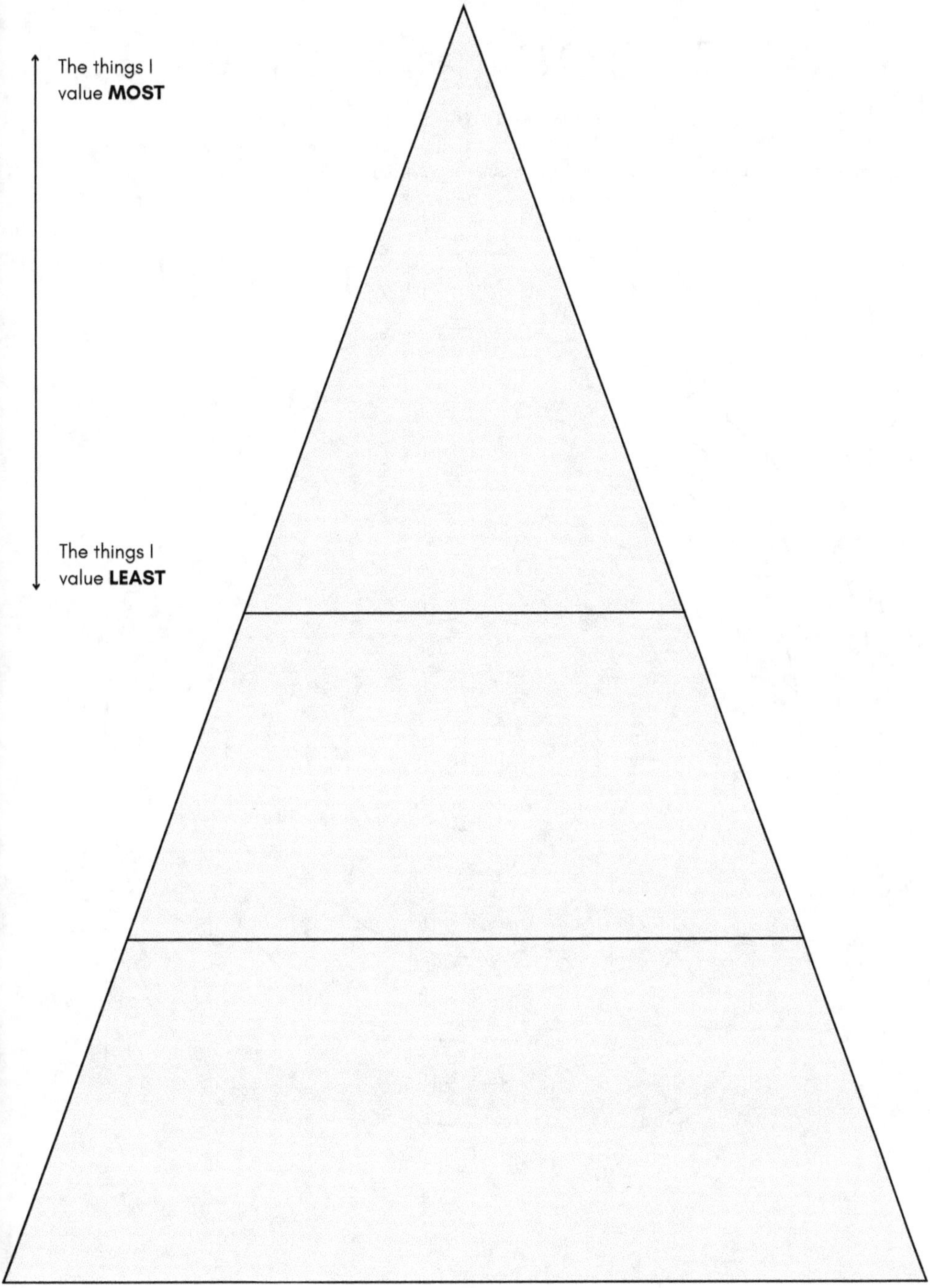

↑ The things I value **MOST**

↓ The things I value **LEAST**

WHEEL OF LIFE

WHERE YOUR MONEY GOES

Use the wheel of life to help you understand where you spend your money. Think about the 8 life categories below, and rate them from 1 - 10. 1 represents you don't spend any money at all in this area, and 10 indicates you spend a lot of money in this area of your life.

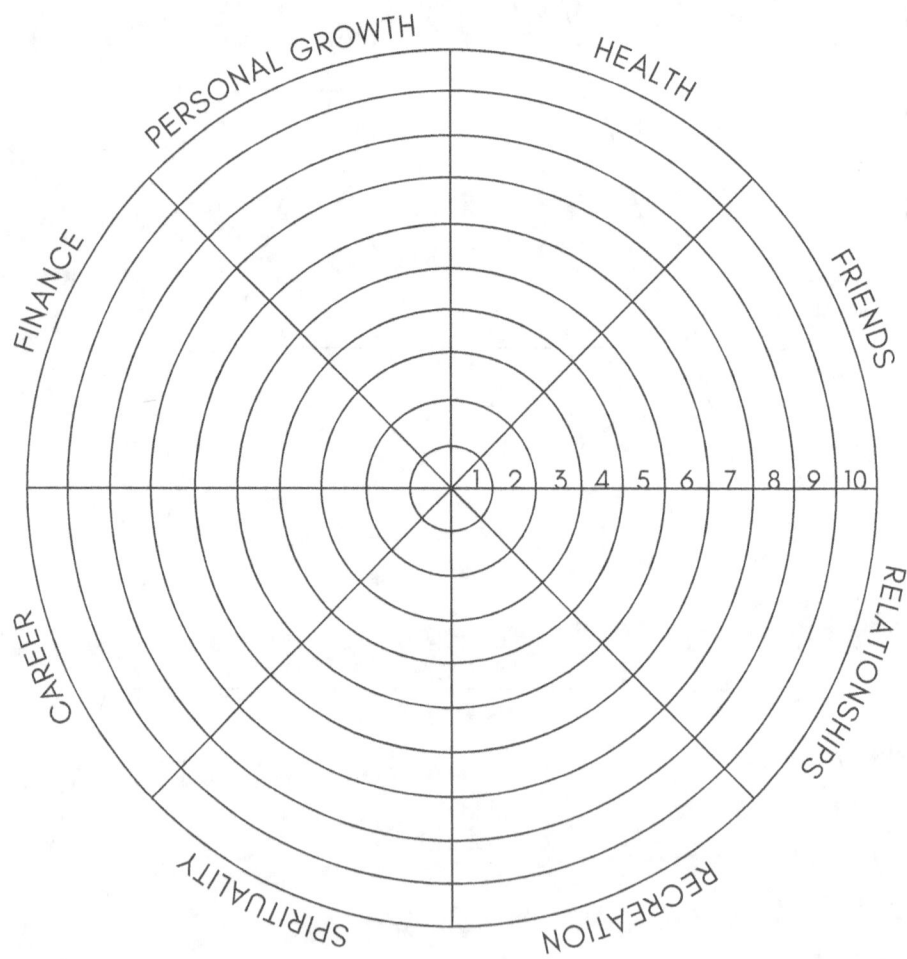

Identifying Your Values

In identify what you value, have a look at your room, your desk space and your web browsing history. For every time you find, place it under each of these pillars. Identify the top three columns with the most items in them. Prioritise then from 1-3. These are your top three values.

My Top 3 Values

1.
2.
3.

Your Money Story

You may not know this, but you probably have an idea of money means to you and your family. Our money story dictates your relationship with money.

If you're in a household where your parents are always fighting about money and not having enough, you might think that there's always a lack of money in your life. As a result, having 'enough' money may be a constant stress for you, and it may lead you to be very conservative about the risks you take. It may also cause additional stress if you have a financial setback.

In contrast, you might grow up in a home where money is abundant and your parents never seem to worry about money. And where the family needed to buy something, there was a plan to save for it. Growing up in a home like this may not trigger stress for you if there's a financial set back. It may encourage you to find alternative solutions to make more money rather than worrying about it. Once we identify our money story, it'll be easier to understand why we treat our money the way we do.

Reflection:

Think about how you talk about money amongst your friends and family. What are the reoccurring themes?

Do you find there's never enough? Or do you always manage to find what you need?

UNDERSTANDING
YOUR MONEY STORY

Let's explore your money story a little further.
Answer the following questions.

WHAT DO YOU KNOW ABOUT MONEY?

WHAT DID YOUR PARENTS TEACH YOU ABOUT MONEY?

DOES MONEY COME EASY TO YOU OR IS IT SCARCE?

WHAT DO YOU DO WHEN YOU EARN AND RECEIVE MONEY?

"NEVER SPEND YOUR MONEY BEFORE YOU HAVE IT." -THOMAS JEFFERSON

Reframe Money Mindset

When it comes to money and life, your mindset can influence how quickly you achieve your goals. If your money story puts you in scarcity mode when it comes to your finances, use this exercise to reframe your money mindset.

Mindset Example	Mental Reframe
I don't have enough money.	Money comes to me when I need it.
I can't afford it.	
I don't have support from my family.	
I don't know how to make more money.	
I'm terrible with money.	
I'm not good at budgeting.	
I don't know much about money.	
Money doesn't come easy to me.	
Rich people are not nice.	
I have to sacrifice a lot to make money.	

MONEY MINDSET

MONEY AFFIRMATIONS

It's been backed by science that your words create your reality. If you are skeptical, look about the emoto rice experiment. What you say about money created your reality, so it's important to be mindful of the things you say. If you find yourself speaking negatively about money or lack there of, use these money affirmations to keep you in line with your money goals.

 Money flows easy to me.

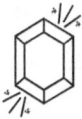 I attract money easily.

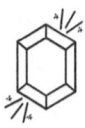 I'm always supported.

 I always have enough.

 I am abundant.

WRITE YOUR OWN
MONEY AFFIRMATIONS

Let's invent new money beliefs
New money beliefs will change your money habits.
Answer the following questions and explore

Examples: Money flows easy to me.
I'm abundant.

CHAPTER TWO

Foundations of
Financial Success

KICKING GOALS

WHY MONEY GOALS MATTER

Having financial goals is like having a map to your dream destination. If you know where you're going, you're more likely to know how you'll get there and what you'll need to do to arrive there.

The secret to sticking to goals is to define your 'why'. Why is it so important to you to meet this goal? What would happen if you achieved it? Use the following prompts to help you define your goals. For each goal you set, ask yourself the following questions.

How much money would you like to have in your bank account in the next 12 months?

Why does having this sum matter to you?

How would having this sum change your life?

SMART

GOAL #1

Let's start your financial journey by setting three goals. To ensure that our goals are specific and achievable, we'll use the SMART goals template, keeping in mind the exercise we did on the previous page.

S	**SPECIFIC** WHAT DO I WANT TO ACCOMPLISH?	
M	**MEASURABLE** HOW WILL I KNOW WHEN IT IS ACCOMPLISHED?	
A	**ACHIEVABLE** HOW CAN THE GOAL BE ACCOMPLISHED?	
R	**RELEVANT** DOES THIS SEEM WORTHWHILE?	
T	**TIME BOUND** WHEN CAN I ACCOMPLISH THIS GOAL?	

SMART
GOAL #2

	SPECIFIC WHAT DO I WANT TO ACCOMPLISH?	
S		

	MEASURABLE HOW WILL I KNOW WHEN IT IS ACCOMPLISHED?	
M		

	ACHIEVABLE HOW CAN THE GOAL BE ACCOMPLISHED?	
A		

	RELEVANT DOES THIS SEEM WORTHWHILE?	
R		

	TIME BOUND WHEN CAN I ACCOMPLISH THIS GOAL?	
T		

SMART

GOAL #3

S	**SPECIFIC** WHAT DO I WANT TO ACCOMPLISH?	
M	**MEASURABLE** HOW WILL I KNOW WHEN IT IS ACCOMPLISHED?	
A	**ACHIEVABLE** HOW CAN THE GOAL BE ACCOMPLISHED?	
R	**RELEVANT** DOES THIS SEEM WORTHWHILE?	
T	**TIME BOUND** WHEN CAN I ACCOMPLISH THIS GOAL?	

BUILD IT

YOUR FINANCIAL VOCABULARLY

DEBT

Debt is money that you owe to someone else, either through a credit card or a personal loan. It's like borrowing money from a friend, but instead, you borrow from a bank, a credit card company, or another lender. When you take on debt, you need to pay back the money you borrowed, usually with an additional amount called interest. Examples of debt include student loans, car loans, credit card balances.

INTEREST

Interest is the extra money you either earn or pay when you borrow or lend money. When you save money in a bank account, the bank gives you interest as an incentive for letting them use your money. If you borrow money through a loan or a credit card, you have to pay interest to the lender. Interest is a percentage of the amount of money you borrowed, and it's added to the total amount you owe. When you borrow money, you not only have to pay back the original amount you borrowed but also the additional interest. Something you bought at a discount may end up costing you much more if you bought it on credit.

BUILD IT

YOUR FINANCIAL VOCABULARLY

CREDIT

Credit is like a financial trust that allows you to borrow money or buy things now and pay for them later. When you use credit (through a credit card), you're using money you may not actually have.

CREDIT SCORE

A credit score is a report card of how well you manage your bills. It tells lenders how likely you are to repay your debts on time. This helps banks determine whether they should lend you money for things like a mortgage. A credit score is built over time and is built from the bills and debt you pay.

CURRENCY

Currency refers to the type of money that is used in a specific country. It's the coins and bills that we use to buy things. Each country has its own coins and notes. In the United States, the currency is the US dollar ($), and in Europe, it's the euro (€). Note that each country's dollar is valued differently so $1 US dollar may only equal to .91 Euros. This exchange rate can change on a daily basis.

BUILD IT

YOUR FINANCIAL VOCABULARLY

OVERDRAFT

An overdraft occurs when you spend more money than you have available in your bank account. The bank covers the difference when there isn't enough money in your account. For example, if you have $50 in your account but need to buy something that costs $70, the bank may allow you to make the purchase by granting you an overdraft of $20.

INFLATION

Inflation is the increase in prices of goods and services over time. It means that things tend to get more expensive as time goes on. Because of inflation a candy bar today will cost a lot more than it did a decade ago.

DIVERSIFICATION

Diversification is a strategy of 'not putting all your eggs in one basket'. It's the action of spreading your investments across different types of assets or investments to reduce risk. People using this strategy will often invest in real estate, stock, and cryptocurrencies to reduce their risk in losing all of their money.

FURTHER READING

RESOURCE LIST

Interested in learning more about financial basics? Here's a list of recommended reading.

Rich Dad Poor Dad - Robert Kiyosaki

Think and Grow Rich - Napoleon Hill

The Total Money Makeover - Dave Ramsey

The Millionaire Next Door - Thomas J. Stanley and William D. Danko

I Will Teach You to Be Rich - by Ramit Sethi

The Money Book for the Young, Fabulous & Broke - Suze Orman

The Teen's Guide to Personal Finance - Joshua Holmberg and David Bruzzese

Get a Financial Life: Personal Finance in Your Twenties and Thirties - Beth Kobliner

The Simple Path to Wealth - JL Collins

Smart Money Smart Kids - Dave Ramsey and Rachel Cruze

The Little Book of Common Sense Investing - John C. Bogle

CHAPTER THREE

Budgeting and Managing Expenses

BUDGETING

MANAGE YOUR FINANCES

When it comes to building wealth, the principle is easy. Don't spend more than what you make. But it's often easier said than done. Setting financial goals is critical if you want to build a nest egg that will set you up nicely for your future. It's why we spent time in the first chapter identifying what matters to you. Once you know what how your money can help you achieve your goals, it'll be much easier to stick to them, especially when you're tempting to splash out on a fancy dinner two weekends in a row.

CREATE YOUR FIRST BUDGET

A budget is a set a amount of money you put aside for everyday expenses, investments and what you'd like to save. Without a budget, you're more likely to spend the money left over in your account.

When you set a budget, start by listing all your monthly expenses, make a record of how they are paid e.g cash, debit, credit. That way you can organise any direct debits so no bill comes at a shock. You'll also want to make note of yearly expenses that amount to a big sum e.g. gym membership paid yearly, car insurance...etc. Breaking up the large sum of payment into monthly chunks can make paying the bill a lot less daunting. Use the following sheet to track your monthly expenses.

expense tracker

MONTH OF

DATE	ITEM	SPENT	REMAINS

Total

NOTES

Spending Tracker

DATE	DESCRIPTION	AMOUNT	CASH	CARD
			○	○
			○	○
			○	○
			○	○
			○	○
			○	○
			○	○
			○	○
			○	○
			○	○
			○	○
			○	○
			○	○
			○	○
			○	○
			○	○
			○	○
			○	○
			○	○
			○	○
			○	○
			○	○
			○	○
			○	○
			○	○

Money Reflection

Now that you've listed all your expenses, can you think of ways to cut back?

Where I'm spending most of my money
_____
_____
_____
_____

Where I can cut back?
_____
_____
_____
_____

Notes

Money Reflection

What are my needs vs wants?
_____
_____
_____
_____
_____

What are my must haves?
_____
_____
_____
_____
_____

Notes

"A BUDGET IS TELLING YOU WHERE
YOUR MONEY IS GOING RATHER THAN
WONDERING WHERE IT WENT."
–DAVE RAMSEY

MONTHLY BUDGET PLANNER

Budget Goal: _____   Month: _____

Income

Date	Description	Amount
Total		

Fixed Expenses

Date	Description	Amount
Total		

Other Expenses

Date	Description	Amount
Total		

Bills

Date	Description	Amount
Total		

Recap

	Goal	Actual	Difference
Earnt			
Spent			
Debt			
Saved			

LONG TERM VS SHORT TERM SATISFACTION

We live in a consumer culture where we're expected to buy stuff, dispose of it, and buy more stuff. That quirky gadget you didn't need but only costs $19 may give you instant satisfaction for a few hours but it'll also set you back from your financial goals by $19.

If you're serious about building wealth, it's important to let your money work for you. So next time you're tempted to buy a shiny new toy that 'only' costs $9, think if you really need it. This is especially true with fast fashion, a new top may only cost $11.99 but you're probably only going to wear it a few times for the next few months and then it's gone. Whereas, if you were to put $11.99 each time you were tempted to buy a top into an investment like a ETF, those small
Lump sums of $11.99 could amount to $100s overtime.

Let's say you passed up five opportunities to buy something (e.g. takeaway, a juice, a comic book) at $9.99. You've saved about $50. Not let's pretend you put the $50 away into something like an index fund that gives you a return of 7%. If you kept the money there for 10 years, the $50 you initially put in would amount to $98.36. That's almost double your money without you having to do much.

OUT OF SIGHT OUT OF MIND

If you see money in your account, it's tempting to spend it. The best way to manage your finances is to allocate a 'job' for every dollar you earn. This could be putting aside $100 into an emergency savings account, $100 for your monthly bills and then $100 for your investments. To avoid the temptation of spending money on things that don't align with your goals, consider having a separate account for:

- Everyday spending: for your day to day transactions like lunch, coffee with friends, transportation costs
- Emergency savings account: for a rainy day and unexpected expenses. Aim to have at least 3 months worth of expenses covered
- Investment account: we'll get into different ways you can invest your money later, but set aside an amount you'd like to invest every month
- Fun money account: budgeting and finances don't need to be boring. Set aside money for splurges, holiday or just to have fun!

MANAGING DEBT

It's no surprise that we live in a buy now, pay later culture. In Australia, companies like Afterpay make it so easy to buy a new phone, pair of sneakers with money we don't have. And eventhough their big sales pitch is that you don't need to pay interest, you do pay in other ways.

Buying things with money you don't have can leave you accumulating a mountain of debt. Not only can it hurt your credit score, it can also cause tremendous stress to your mental health. When possible, always pay for things upfront.

CREDIT IS A DOUBLE EDGE SWORD

There's a good and bad side to credit. On one hand, buying things on credit is great if you have a credit card that lets you collect airline miles, you'd like to build your credit score or you'd like to free up your cash flow. But it's only a great tool if you can pay your bills off every month. This is where the downside of credit comes in.

Credit card companies often charge a high interest rate, typically at 18%. That can add up to a lot of money if you have hundreds or thousands of dollars to pay back. Let's have a look at an example. Let's say your favourite artist is performing in your town and you'd like to buy VIP tickets. They cost about $800. You don't get paid for another 30 days so you'd like to purchase the tickets on your credit card.

Now let's say you don't pay the card off. Here's how the numbers look:

$800 on credit card
18% interest rate
If monthly payments were $39/month and you took two years to pay it off, you'd pay an extra $144. If you took five years and two months paying $20/month, you'd pay $431 in interest

GOOD DEBT VS BAD DEBT

Not all debt is bad. The previous example showed that buying on credit could end up costing more if you don't have the funds to pay it off in 21 days. But there are situations where debt could be a positive thing. The general rule of thumb is- if you're using debt to make more money, it's worth looking into. This goes for real estate, investing in property or even a stock portfolio. Some of these items require significant investment you may not already have and it's common to look to lenders like your bank for assistance.

How to reduce debt and pay it off quickly

In our credit card example, you saw just how much interest can add up if you can't pay back your balance. If you have credit card debt and want to reduce it quickly, aim to see if you can transfer your balance into a credit card with a lower interest rate. Look to taking a personal loan with a smaller interest. And if you're struggling to pay your bills on time, speak to your credit card company, many are understating.

CHAPTER FOUR

Earning Money and Building Wealth

INVESTING FUNDAMENTALS

TYPES OF INVESTMENTS

When it comes to building wealth, a get rich quick strategy does not exist. Though, if someone promises you this, run the other way. The technology we have today allows us to do so much but it's also given scammers a lot of opportunity to take advantage of it.

The most positive thing is that you have time on your side to take risks, learn from your mistakes and try again. Make educated guesses in all your investments but don't be afraid to make mistakes- it's the best way to learn. Before you invest, it's always best to speak to a qualified financial planner and accountant. Here are a few ways to invest your money. Everyone will have their own preferences, and as you learn about them, you'll get to know which is right for you.

When looking for an investment, you'll likely want to opt for a long term strategy rather than make a quick buck. This will influence how you want to approach the following investment ideas

INVESTMENT IDEA #1

STOCKS

Difficulty to learn
4 stars out of 5

Investing in stocks is one of the easiest ways to get into investing. You can start with little capital if you do your research. But whether you succeed depends on how much time you have to dedicate to research companies and their earning potential. Most experts like the idea of stocks that pay investors dividends. This can be a great way to generate passive incomes as a sum is paid to investors when a company turns a profit.

If you choose to buy individual stocks, the risk can be high if you're a beginner. Some experts advise to start with steady companies you know like banks.

The stock market can be volatile as it's influenced by world events, always invest what you can afford to lose.

Practice first with a training account
If you want to try your hand at investing in stocks, most trading platforms have training accounts that stimulate live accounts. You can practice trading without using your own money to begin with.

INVESTMENT IDEA #1

How to get started:

- Either chat to your bank's investment broker or look into trading platforms in your country. Just make sure you read the reviews to ensure the sites are legitimate.
- Once you've opened an account, you'll need to deposit your funds before you can trade

INVESTMENT IDEA #2

INDEX FUNDS

Difficulty to learn
4 stars out of 5

Index funds are a type of mutual fund or exchange-traded fund (ETF) that mimics the performance of a specific market index, such as the S&P 500 or the Dow Jones Industrial Average.

Think of index funds as a collection of stocks that represent a particular segment of the overall stock market. The S&P 500 index for example is a collection of the 500 largest publicly traded companies in the United States.

Index funds are great if you don't have a lot of budget to buy individual stocks. For example, a stock at a major bank may go for $50 per share but you may only have $100 to invest. Buy investing in an ETF, you can own a small portion of the company in the index.

Index funds are popular among investors at all skill levels because they offer diversification. Rather than investing in one business, you're putting your money. in many companies you may not have access to on a limited budget.

INVESTMENT IDEA #2

Index funds are often recommended for long-term investing and building wealth over time. It's a great option for beginners as it requires a lot less time in research.

How to get started:

- Do your research on ETF funds. Vanguard is a popular one to look into but you'll need to do your own research to find the best one for you
- Once you've opened an account, you'll need to deposit your funds before you can invest

INVESTMENT IDEA #3

REAL ESTATE

Difficulty to learn
4 stars out of 5

Investing in real estate often requires a minimum of 10% deposit. Depending on the location you choose to invest, a lump sum of funds isn't always accessible to everyone. For that reason alone , it gets a rating of four stars.

If budget is not an issue, you'll need to spend time getting to know the suburbs, its growth potential, and the prime streets to look out for. The great thing about investing in real estate is that it's a tangible asset. Also in any market, people will always need a place to live.

How to get started:

- Start by following listings for sale/for rent so you. can learn the market
- Speak to local Real Estate agents and brokers to see what inventory is available

INVESTMENT IDEA #4

START/BUY A BUSINESS

Difficulty to learn
4 stars out of 5

If you are interested in owning a business, starting your own or buying one may be a great option. You'll need to do your research to see if your skills set is compatible with owning a business, the earning potential and how much you'd need to break even. We'll dive deeper into business, passive income and side hustles later on.

How to get started:

- Consider what you'd like to sell
- Do your research into what people are buying right now (consider products that people buy in any market)
- Consider whether you'll build your own business or buy one from a website like EmpireFlippers.com

INVESTMENT IDEA #5

YOUR EDUCATION

Difficulty to learn
*Depends on the subject of interest

Investing in yourself can bump up your earning potential. Don't overlook investing in a course or degree so you can boost your salary or fees you charge.

How to get started:

- Research topics/courses you're interested in
- Consider the potential return of your education either in rates you may be able to charge or things you can create with your new skill
- Contact the educator on pre-requisites required

DEALING WITH MARKET CHANGES

The market changes all the time so if there's one thing to expect, it's that your investments and your return on them will fluctuate. For example, a market downturn could mean house prices can go down 10% a year and then recover the next. If you can learn to thrive in any market you're bound to succeed. So this would be looking into investments that are recession proof. For example, in an economic downturn, people will still need some place to live. Or if you're looking into buying shares, think of things people still buy, necessities like toilet paper.

If you prefer to have a steady income to start, a job may be the best option for you. The following section takes you through landing your first gig.

EARNING MONEY

LANDING YOUR FIRST JOB

Finding your first job can be a scary thought, but it doesn't have to be a scary process.

Your first job probably won't be your "forever" job, but it can open new doors and help you build independence. And let's not forget the most exciting part, that sweet feeling of earning your own money.

If you're like most people looking for their first job, it's not a matter of searching for job tips online (chances are you've spent time on Google already). The tricky part is finding job advice that's actually, ya know, useful.

In this chapter, we'll explore some simple and proven steps to landing your first job. This includes:

- How to find a job that aligns with your values
- Common job options available (and how to apply for them)
- Creative job opportunities on social media (#girlboss)
- Proven interview and resume-writing tips
- Money-making side hustle ideas

Let's dive in and break down everything you need to know to go from stress to success.

EARNING MONEY

HOW TO FIND A JOB THAT ALIGNS WITH YOUR VALUES

What's the first thing you think about when picturing your dream job?

If you're thinking of money, flexible hours, and the chance to work with your friends, we don't blame you (that sounds like a dream job to us too).

But the one thing often overlooked is finding a job that aligns with your values.

Why are values important?

Because you want to enjoy your time at work.

Think of it this way. Imagine sitting in your least favourite class… for hours and hours every day. Talk about pain!

The same thing happens when you land a job that doesn't align with your values. You end up staring at the clock, waiting for every shift to end, and wondering how you ended up here in the first place!

Here's how you find a job that aligns with your values so you can look forward to every shift.

EARNING MONEY

HOW TO FIND A JOB THAT ALIGNS WITH YOUR VALUES

Step One: Get to know yourself and your goals

Before you start firing off CVs and application letters, you have to be honest with yourself about your values. Core values could include teamwork, creativity, diversity, kindness or honesty.

Step Two: Research, research, research

Once you've identified your values, you'll need to research potential companies to ensure they tick your boxes. You can't do this simply by reading job descriptions. Instead, look for reviews and testimonials for an inside look at potential employers.

EARNING MONEY

HOW TO FIND A JOB THAT ALIGNS WITH YOUR VALUES

Step Three: Separate "red flags" from "trade-offs"

Not every job will give you sleep-ins and weekends off, but that doesn't mean they fail the 'Value Test'. Revisit your value list and make sure you're only ruling out a job because it doesn't align with your values, not because they won't let you call in sick after a big Saturday night out with your friends.

Follow this simple framework, and you'll be ready to find a job that adds value to your life.

What's that?

You're not sure where to find job opportunities?!

We thought you might say that. Read on for a few simple and effective ways to find your first job.

WHERE TO FIND (EASY) FIRST JOB OPPORTUNITIES

Finding your first job can be like looking for something to watch on Netflix. There seem to be so many options, but you can search for ages without finding something you like.

And hey, we get it.

Just because you *can* do a job doesn't mean you should. Remember, the right job won't just put money in your bank account (*cha-ching*). It will also align with your values.

To get the ball rolling, here are a few common job ideas for first-time job seekers.

- **Anything close to home:** We're talking about babysitting, dog sitting, lawn mowing, tidying up, washing cars, you get the idea. These are the types of chores most people don't want to do and can help you start building a job history (more on that below).
- **Hospitality:** AI might be the hottest topic, but robots can't help wait tables, clean dishes, take orders, or do any other jobs you'll find in cafes, restaurants and other service businesses. Hospitality jobs help build valuable skills that future employers will look for. Also, did someone say cash tips?!

Retail: We're not just saying this for potential discounts on cute outfits (even if that is a nice benefit). Retail jobs can help you kickstart your employment and don't require extensive experience, so you can learn on the job and build up your skillset (and maybe your wardrobe too).

Social Media: Do you have an engaged social media following who hangs on every word and post? You don't need 1 million+ followers to be an influencer. Whether you're on IG, TikTok, Snapchat or YouTube, an engaged audience can be the start of a personal brand. From brand partnerships to sponsored posts, it all starts by cultivating an audience (of any size) who trusts your recommendations.

Got your eye on a specific industry or role?

Awesome!

There are plenty of ways to apply for the job you want, so don't feel you need to drop resumes in by hand (even if your parents hit you with, "That's how we did it in my day!").

Here are a few go-to ways to apply for a job:

- Search for 'entry level' positions on online job boards like Indeed and SEEK.
- Research businesses you'd like to work for to look for job openings and send an email.
- Ask friends or family for any contacts or referrals who might be looking for new staff.

HOW TO WRITE A RESUME (EVEN IF YOU HAVE NO EXPERIENCE)

Most articles online will tell you to "highlight your experience" when it comes to writing a resume, which is great advice... unless you don't have any experience!

You're writing a resume for your first job, so chances are you won't have much (or any) work experience to show off. But don't stress, there are a few simple ways to put your best foot forward and impress potential employers.

Here are a few proven strategies to help your CV land on top of the pile:

Highlight your education: Adding your education can help show your interests, passions and strengths. This could be a specific course or program you've completed or simply your school or university success up until now.

Include relevant experience: Maybe you've worked a part-time job, volunteered, or spent weekends helping your grandma mow her lawn (we say that counts as a "casual gardener", so add it to the CV). Showing a relevant work history is powerful, even if your work history is thin.

List your skills: Are you a wiz on Instagram? You've got social media skills. Do you often take the lead on school projects? You've got leadership skills. Don't add qualities for the sake of it, but think of relevant skills you use in your daily life. Other examples might include public speaking, research or communication.

BONUS TIP: A single-page cover letter can help your resume stand out. Your resume explains your experience, and your cover letter explains why you're a good fit for the job. Keep your cover letter short and to the point while emphasizing why you're a great fit for the job.

It's OK to feel nervous writing a resume without real-life work experience. Just remember, employers hire people, not pieces of paper. Your resume's job is to get attention, put your best foot forward, and show your future boss what you bring to the table.

Once you get to the interview, that's when you'll show off what a great employee you'd make.

Speaking of interviews...

5 "NAIL THE INTERVIEW" TIPS TO HELP YOU STAND OUT

#1 - Brush up on the company: Learning a little about the business is a surefire way to build your confidence. Spend 10-15 minutes learning about the company's big-picture mission and the products/services they sell to show you've done your homework.

#2 - Practice your answers: You'll likely be asked questions like, "Tell me about yourself", "What are your strengths and weaknesses?", and "Why should we hire you?". Practising your answers will help soothe the nerves and turn an interview into a casual conversation.

#3 - Ask questions: Remember, you're not the only one being interviewed; you also need to make sure the business is right for you! Try asking about what an average day looks like, what challenges you'll face, and what is expected of an employee to get a feel for the role.

#4 - Dress to impress: We're not saying you should throw on a ballgown, but wear suitable clothing that says, "Hey, I'm professional, and I'm serious about this role". Studies have shown verbal content makes up just 7% of a first impression, so don't underestimate what a great outfit can do.

#5 - Be your (best) self: It's OK to feel nervous about a job interview, but whether you land the job or not won't be the end of the world. Go in with the plan to be your best self - that means good posture, making eye contact, and engaging with your interviewer. If you do that, you can hold your head high no matter what happens.

There's no perfect way to find, apply for, and land your first job. So don't feel like you're doing anything "wrong" if the process takes time or stresses you out.

Whatever job you get can become an important part of your life, but it will never be your entire life.

Work your way through the tips in this chapter, and you'll be waking up, clocking in, and getting paid for your first job in no time.

Happy job hunting!!!

Your Job Planner

Now that you know what steps to take to land your first gig, let's reflect and come up with a plan to get your dream job.

What am I interested in?
_____
_____
_____
_____
_____

What jobs are available with my skills set?
_____
_____
_____
_____
_____

Job Ideas

CHAPTER FIVE

Passive Income and Entrepreneurship

PASSIVE INCOME

We live in a decade where opportunities to earn a living online and in person are everywhere. Your parents may have lived in a generation where the status quo was to get a good education, get a job, and then buy a home. But thanks to technology, your journey can be so much more exciting.

There are plenty of businesses you can start with as little as $100. Ready to channel your inner Kim Kardashian and flex those girl boss muscles?

The key to finding a great side hustle is to find something that won't eat all of your free time. By creating a side hustle around something you actually enjoy, you'll be able to earn money without feeling like you're missing out on life.

Before we get into business ideas and passive income, we need to set some expectations. For one, true passive income doesn't exist unless you're investing in real estate of ETFs. And even those types of investment require some set up time to make it work. The reality is that most passive income business ideas will require you to put in time or money. But the idea is that the time you spend on it is a lot less than you'd spend in a traditional job.

10 SIDE HUSTLE IDEAS

Here are a few creative side hustle ideas to help you earn some extra money.

1. Print on Demand

A business model that lets you sell physical products without holding any inventory. You can create designs for tote bags, t-shirts and blankets to upload into a store or marketplace like Etsy.

Pros: Little start up costs
Cons: It's a competitive market
Resources:
- Printify.com
- YouTube.com/wholesaleted

2. Dropshipping

If you like the idea of holding zero inventory but have no design skills, dropshipping may be a great option for you. How it works is that you choose a few products to sell, sell them via social media or your own website and once someone places an order, you place the order with your supplier. They then ship the product straight to your customers.

Pros: Zero inventory, easy to start with a limited budget
Cons: You don't have much control over shipping and packaging
Resources:
- Aliexpress.com
- Oberlo.com

3. Affiliate Marketing

If you like the thought of promoting other people's courses or products, affiliate marketing is also beginner friendly. How it works is that you choose a product and create content to promote it via channels like YouTube, TikTok, Pinterest. When someone places an order with your link, you get a commission.

Pros: Little start-up costs, the potential for high commissions
Cons: Building traffic to your content can take a long time to establish
Resources:
- affiliate-program.amazon.com

4. Content Creation

If you're not shy in front of the camera, have an artistic flare and love social media, content creation may be a great income stream for you. Select a topic you're interested, build a following and partner with brand on sponsored content or ambassadorships.

Pros: Low barrier to enter, most start as a hobby
Cons: Building an audience takes a lot of time unless you get lucky and have a piece of content go viral.

5. Online Course Creator

IDo you have a special skill you can teach? Whether it's piano, woodworking or design skills, course creators can make a healthy income teaching others online.

Pros: You can create courses online meaning that you'd only need to do the work once while seeing a return for as long as your course is on sale.

Cons: It can take a lot of time to film and create the content. You'll also need to put some effort into marketing your course.

Resources:
- Udemy.com
- Teachable.com

6. Content Creation

If you like the thought of promoting other people's courses or products, affiliate marketing is also beginner friendly. How it works is that you choose a product and create content to promote it via channels like YouTube, TikTok, Pinterest. When someone places an order with your link, you get a commission.

Pros: Little start-up costs, the potential for high commissions
Cons: Building traffic to your content can take a long time to establish
Resources:
- affiliate-program.amazon.com

7. Virtual Assistant

Are you great with technology? If the idea of helping small businesses, a gig as a virtual assistant may be a right fit. Every day may be different and you might find yourself creating social media posts, doing admin work or sending following emails to customers.

Pros: You're likely to earn a steady wage while engaged with the project.
Cons: You might miss face time with your boss or colleagues as everything is done online.
Resources:
- Fivver.com
- Upwork.com

8. Pet Minding

Are you in love with every pup you see? If you're an animal lover, you can make money taking care of people's furry or feathered friends while they're away.

Pros: No cost to set up if you use social media and word of mouth
Cons: Requires experience in working with pets, you'll also need to look into buying insurance

9. Tutoring

Helping other students improve their grades can be a great way to make extra cash if you enjoy teaching others. Try asking around your friend group, or get your parents to check in with their friends.

Pros: You can charge above minimum wage
Cons: Since you'll be trading time for a wage, there's a limit to how many students you can tutor

10. **Food Delivery**

If you've got your own transportation (or a car you can borrow), you can deliver food for companies like UberEats, DoorDash or MenuLog. You'll need to be 18+ to land this gig, but it means you can also blast your tunes while you work. And that's it!

Pros: It's flexible, you can work whenever you want
Cons: You'll need a vehicle

A DEDICATED
IDEAS DUMP

Use the following pages to write down all
the business ideas you can think of

REFLECTION

THOUGHTS

Now that you've put all your business ideas down, it's time to narrow in on the ones that really resonate with you.

Write a short list of businesses you'd be most interested in building.

- _____
- _____
- _____
- _____
- _____
- _____
- _____
- _____

REFLECTION

YOUR TOP 3 IDEAS

From your short list of business ideas, choose 3 based on the following criteria: 1. Cost to build the business 2. Investment in time 3. Time from idea to launch.

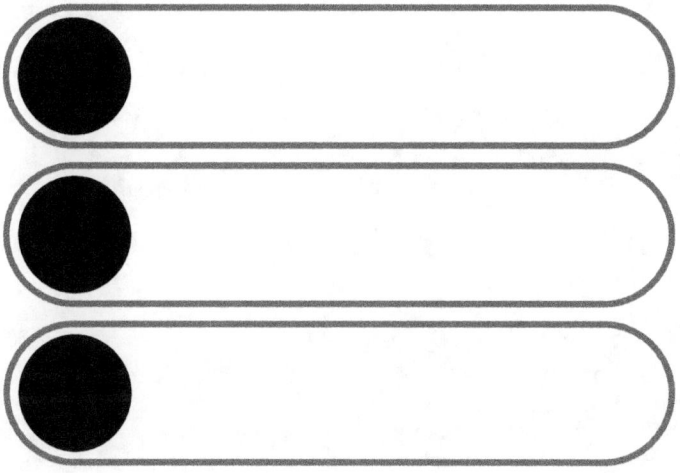

Time to get feedback! Chat through your top 3 ideas with a friend or your parents.

BUSINESS IDEA #1

You've honed in on 3 business ideas. It's time to decide on one.

Question 1: Is there a demand for your product/service?

-
-
-

Question 2: How much could you potentially make?

-
-
-

Question 3: How easy/difficult is this idea for you to execute?

-
-
-

BUSINESS IDEA #2

You've honed in on 3 business ideas. It's time to decide on one.

Question 1: Is there a demand for your product/service?

-
-
-

Question 2: How much could you potentially make?

-
-
-

Question 3: How easy/difficult is this idea for you to execute?

-
-
-

BUSINESS IDEA #3

You've honed in on 3 business ideas. It's time to decide on one.

Question 1: Is there a demand for your product/service?

-
-
-

Question 2: How much could you potentially make?

-
-
-

Question 3: How easy/difficult is this idea for you to execute?

-
-
-

CHAPTER SIX

Money Challenges

"WEALTH IS NOT ABOUT HAVING A LOT OF MONEY. IT'S ABOUT HAVING OPTIONS"
-CHRIS ROCK

FUN WITH MONEY

MONEY CHALLENGES

If you've made it to this part of the book, you've come on a big journey. Money and learning about money doesn't have to be serious and boring.

In fact, it can be challenging and fun. The following pages contain a series of money challenges you. can do with a friend. Whether. you opt for the 30 day or 100 day challenge, there's a page for each of you to complete.

M$NEY P$T

SAVINGS TRACKER

Amount: _____   Goal date: _____

SAVINGS TRACKER

SAVING FOR ....
START DATE ....
AMOUNT ....
GOAL DATE ....

SAVINGS TRACKER

SAVING FOR ....

START DATE ....

AMOUNT ....

GOAL DATE ....

SAVINGS TRACKER
Money pot

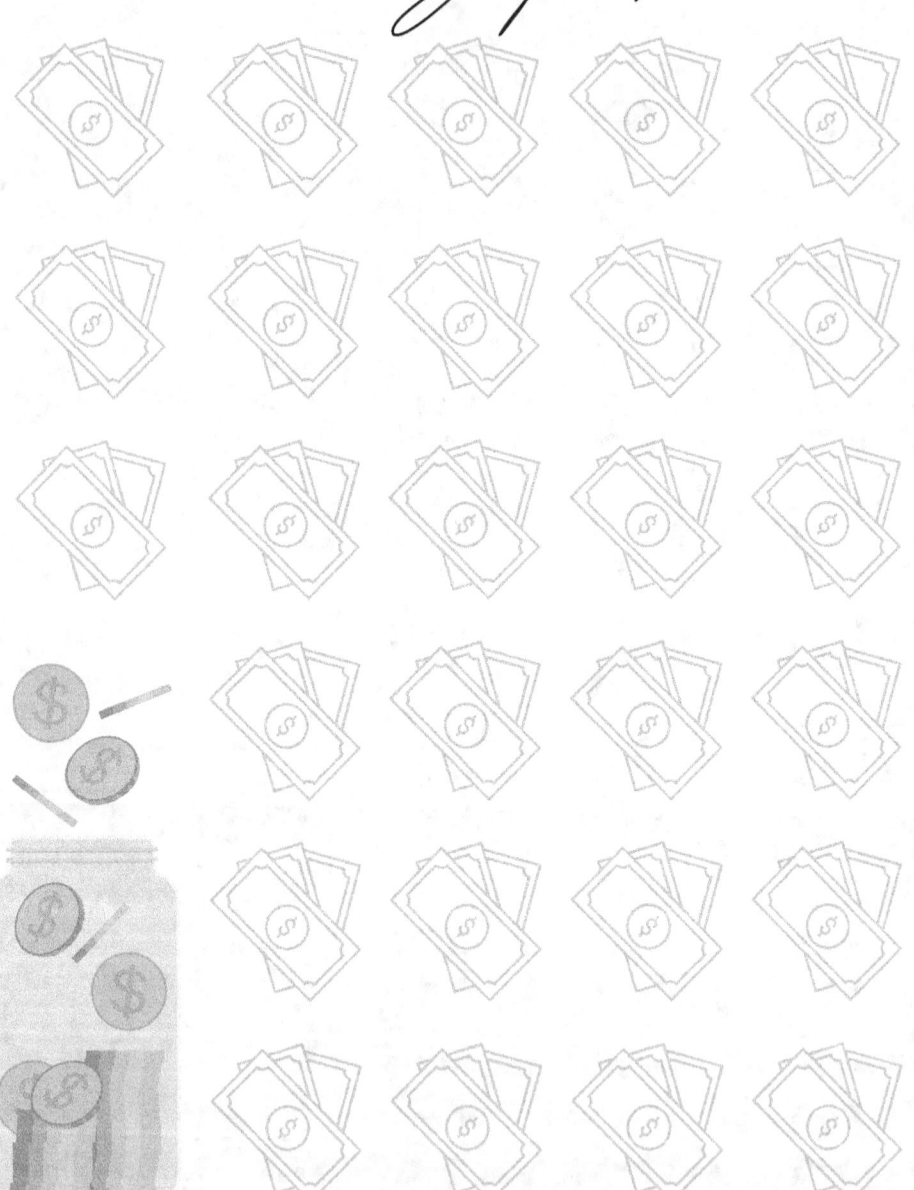

SAVINGS TRACKER
Money pot

100 DAYS CHALLENGE

TARGET	

1	2	3	4	5	6	7	8	9	10
11	12	13	14	15	16	17	18	19	20
21	22	23	24	25	26	27	28	29	30
31	32	33	34	35	36	37	38	39	40
41	42	43	44	45	46	47	48	49	50
51	52	53	54	55	56	57	58	59	60
61	62	63	64	65	66	67	68	69	70
71	72	73	74	75	76	77	78	79	80
81	82	83	84	85	86	87	88	89	90
91	92	93	94	95	96	97	98	99	100

NOTE

100 DAYS CHALLENGE

TARGET	

1	2	3	4	5	6	7	8	9	10
11	12	13	14	15	16	17	18	19	20
21	22	23	24	25	26	27	28	29	30
31	32	33	34	35	36	37	38	39	40
41	42	43	44	45	46	47	48	49	50
51	52	53	54	55	56	57	58	59	60
61	62	63	64	65	66	67	68	69	70
71	72	73	74	75	76	77	78	79	80
81	82	83	84	85	86	87	88	89	90
91	92	93	94	95	96	97	98	99	100

NOTE

30 DAYS
$200 Challenge

$10	$1	$5	$9	$7
$4	$13	$2	$6	$8
$5	$1	$10	$12	$4
$3	$10	$12	$5	$8
$11	$14	$3	$15	$7
$12	$1	$6	$4	$2

CONGRATULATIONS!

30 DAYS
$200 Challenge

$10	$1	$5	$9	$7
$4	$13	$2	$6	$8
$5	$1	$10	$12	$4
$3	$10	$12	$5	$8
$11	$14	$3	$15	$7
$12	$1	$6	$4	$2

CONGRATULATIONS!

NO SPEND CHALLENGE

1	2	3	4	5	6
7	8	9	10	11	12
13	14	15	16	17	18
19	20	21	22	23	24
25	26	27	28	29	30

31 — YOU DID IT!

NOTES

_____
_____
_____
_____

NO SPEND CHALLENGE

1	2	3	4	5	6
7	8	9	10	11	12
13	14	15	16	17	18
19	20	21	22	23	24
25	26	27	28	29	30

31 — YOU DID IT!

NOTES

WHAT'S NEXT?

NEXT STEPS

CONTINUE LEARNING

Learning about money and honing any skill takes time and resilience. There's no doubt that you'll make mistakes along the way but you'll learn from them and get smarter with your money.

If you're interested in getting your family involved in budget planner and improving your finances, I have a family budget planner. If you'd like a copy, please send an email to iona@prettypicklesshop.com with the subject headering: Family Budget Planner.

PERSONAL DEVELOPMENT
OTHER BOOKS

If you liked this book, you may enjoy others like it:

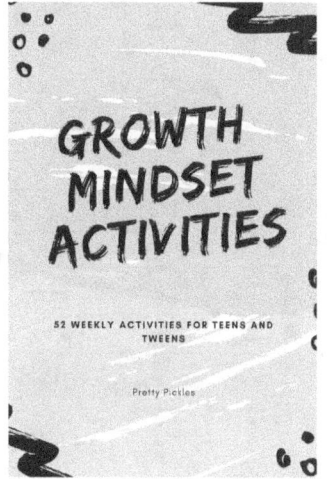
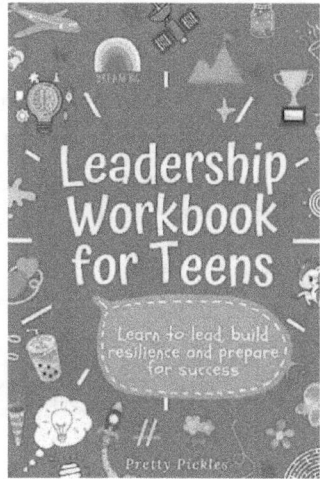

NOTES

Date:

NOTES

Date:

www.ingramcontent.com/pod-product-compliance
Lightning Source LLC
Chambersburg PA
CBHW070310010526
44107CB00056B/2546